CONTENTS & TRACK LIST

Full Mixes

Backing Tracks

GW00632710

Welcome to book 2!

This is where you jam your way to becoming a better guitarist.

We teach you all the required rudiments to perform successfully in your very **First Audition Grade.**

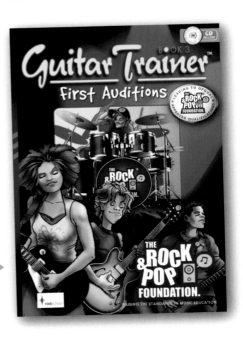

You still have an enjoyable blend of both **Classical and Rock styles to play**, but, most importantly...

You must tackle all the exercises needed to make you into a complete guitar player.

Remember the guitar is a magical as well as a very technical instrument.

Keep the training fluent and you'll enjoy playing FOREVER!

STICK AT IT, WORK HARD, HAVE FUN AND YOU WILL BE THE BEST!

Notes on the 1st string.

E **F** **G**

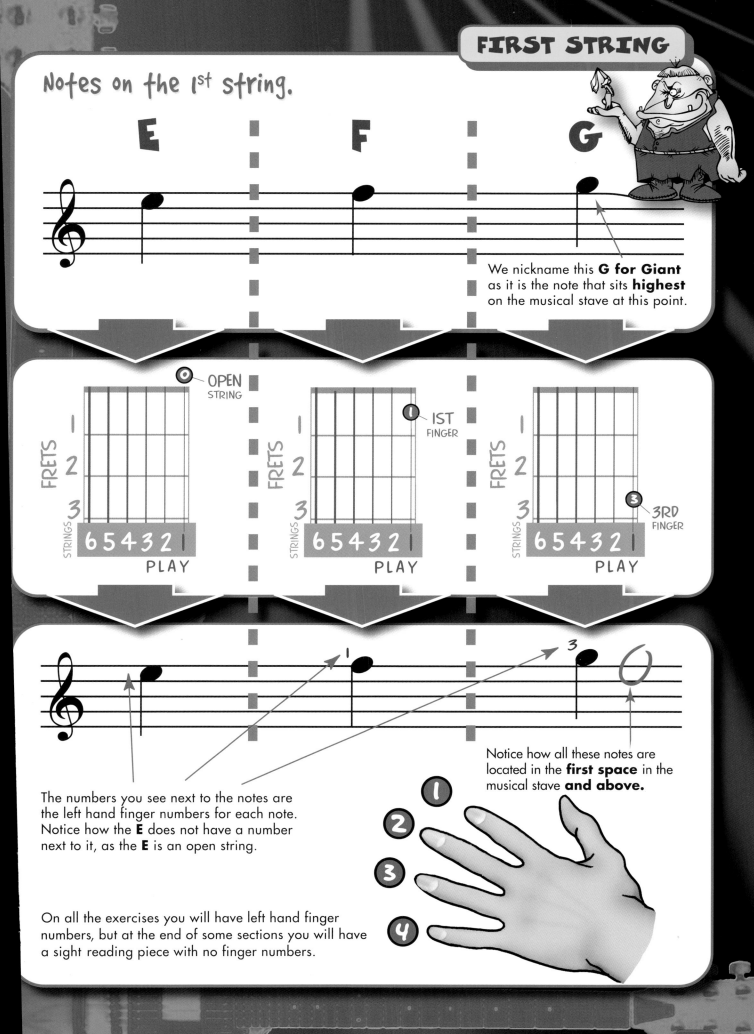

We nickname this **G for Giant** as it is the note that sits **highest** on the musical stave at this point.

○ — OPEN STRING

FRETS 1 2 3
STRINGS
6 5 4 3 2 1
PLAY

① — IST FINGER

FRETS 1 2 3
STRINGS
6 5 4 3 2 1
PLAY

③ — 3RD FINGER

FRETS 1 2 3
STRINGS
6 5 4 3 2 1
PLAY

Notice how all these notes are located in the **first space** in the musical stave **and above.**

The numbers you see next to the notes are the left hand finger numbers for each note. Notice how the **E** does not have a number next to it, as the **E** is an open string.

On all the exercises you will have left hand finger numbers, but at the end of some sections you will have a sight reading piece with no finger numbers.

① ② ③ ④

whole notes.

When looking at a piece of music the first thing we need to study is the **time signature.** Notice all the exercises below are written in **4/4.** This means that all the **notes** and **rests** must add up to **4 beats per bar.**

W is a **whole note** it's worth **4 beats**

Think of the **whole note**...
like an **orange**.

It is a similar shape.

The orange is worth 4 beats.

Count: G   2   3   4

H is a **Half note** it's worth **2 beats**

$$\text{H} + \text{H} = \text{o}$$
$$2 + 2 = 4$$

If you cut the orange in half you have **2 pieces**
Each piece is worth **2 beats**

$$2 + 2 = 4$$

Count: G   2   G   2

G   2   Rest   2

Q is a **Quarter note** only worth **1 beat**

$$\text{Q} + \text{Q} + \text{Q} + \text{Q} = \text{o}$$
$$1+1+1+1 = 4$$

$$1 + 1 + 1 + 1 = 4$$

Count: G   G   G   G   Play what you see.

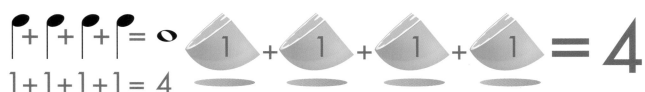

PICK 'N' MIX IT (with the best of them!)

Before you play this piece **clap** through the **notation.**
This will help you to understand the rhythm. We call it **"Pick 'n' Mix It"** because it mixes together all the different types of **notes** and **rests** learnt so far in one piece of music.

RH - WALKING FINGERS

Four String Sprint.

We will now take time to look at a **right hand** workout. It is played on **open strings** to allow you to concentrate only on the **right hand fingers.**

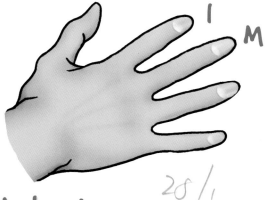

I   M

Walking fingers I & M.

Using walking fingers play each string on the guitar 4 times & time yourself. Next week should be quicker.

Rest your **thumb** on the **6th string** as this will help you to keep your hand in position

28/1

Workout 1.

TAB

I M I M I M I M I M I M I M I M

Time week 1: 12 secs **Time week 2:** 67 secs

Workout 2.

TAB

I M I M I M I M I M I M I M I M

Time week 1: 14 secs **Time week 2:** 77 secs

Notes on the 2nd string.

Here you will find the notes of **B C & D**
We call this **B 'Bang in the Middle'** for two reasons. Notice how the **B** is located **bang in the middle** of the **musical stave** and when you look at **string number two** on your guitar it is **bang in the middle** of strings **1 & 3.**

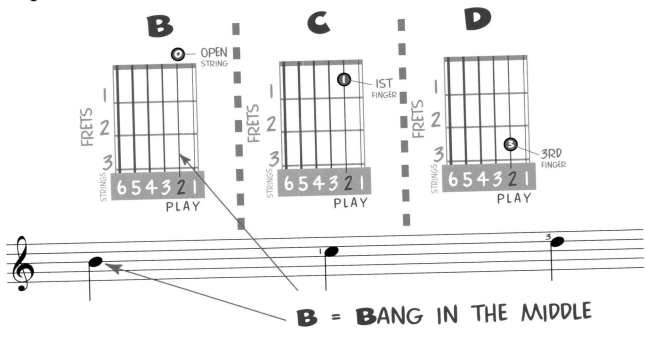

B = BANG IN THE MIDDLE

Session 2.

W is a **whole note** it's worth **4 beats**

count: B   2   3   4

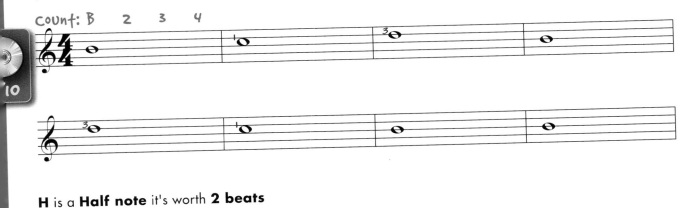

H is a **Half note** it's worth **2 beats**

count: B   2   B   2

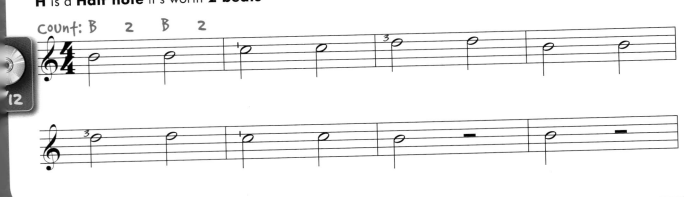

Session 2 (cont.)

Q is a **Quarter note** only worth **1 beat**

BOSSA NOVA

FUNKY LADDER

Here we take a combination of **1st** and **2nd string notes** together in one piece. If you look closely the clue is in the title. The first 2 bars are notes on the **1st string** and climb down to notes on the **2nd string** on bars 3 and 4. The rest is up to you to work out. **Good Luck!**

formula 4 success.

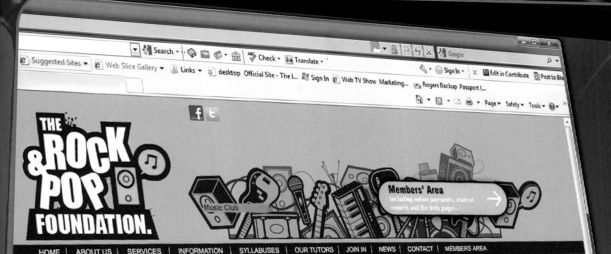

THE ROCK & POP FOUNDATION.

HOME | ABOUT US | SERVICES | INFORMATION | SYLLABUSES | OUR TUTORS | JOIN IN | NEWS | CONTACT | MEMBERS AREA

Members' Area
Including online payments, student reports and the help pages...

Information Home

About Us
About Exams
For Parents
For Schools
For Students
  ↳ Games
For Tutors

JOIN IN
Find out how to get involved with The Rock & Pop Foundation.
CLICK HERE

ENTER HERE

Games

Motor Music

Drive the cars, boats and planes and pick up the notes you're asked for and bonuses along the way but whatever you do, don't hit the wrong notes!

You'll have to be fast to get to them all!

Note Race Relay

Race against the clock to see how fast you can read the notes. You can choose how many you want to answer.

Try racing against your friends to see who's the fastest reader!

Have a rest!

You might know your notes, but what about the rests? They're just as important!

See how fast you can work out how many beats each of the rests that you see are worth

Gen-Duration Game

Do you know your half notes from your quavers?

See how fast you can recognise the different types of notes by cliking on how many beats they're worth choose how many to answer then race against the stopwatch!

More Info And Games At our website

Log in to www.RockAndPopFoundation.com with your personal username and password, then go to 'Students' and 'Online Games'. Here you'll find a number of challenging games to play to quickly improve your music knowledge.

It's great fun too!

Notes on the 3rd string.

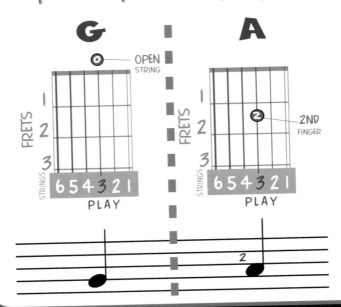

Here you will find the notes of **G** and **A**. This string in the first position has only two notes so within this exercise we shall also look at a different time signature.

We call this **A for Ambulance**. If you play from **A** to **G** and **repeat** it **very fast** it sounds like an ambulance racing down the road!

So far we have looked at the $\frac{4}{4}$ time signature which means **4 beats in a bar.**

This session we will look at the $\frac{3}{4}$ time signature which means **3 beats in a bar.**

The first exercise will give you practise on the notes on the **3rd string** and the second exercise will give you a counting exercise with 3 beat notes.

A dotted half note = 3 beats.

If a **dot** is placed **after** a note it means **add half** the value to the note.

Third string Workout 1.

22

Third string Workout 2.

count: G   2   3

/24

The Jazz Waltz.

The Wacky Waltz has 3 beats in a bar with combinations of **1st, 2nd** and **3rd string** notes. **Remember** to keep the beat **smooth** otherwise your fingers will trip up!

The Waltz is a famous dance.

Twinkle little rock star!

In **bars 1** and **2** make sure you **hold down** the note of **'d'**. The reason for this is to help you **play at speed**. You have **open strings** either side of the **'d'** so you don't have to take your finger off the note. Ensure when you **hold down** the **'d'** on the left hand you have a good **railway tunnel**, otherwise the open strings will **not ring** through.

Notes on the 4th string.

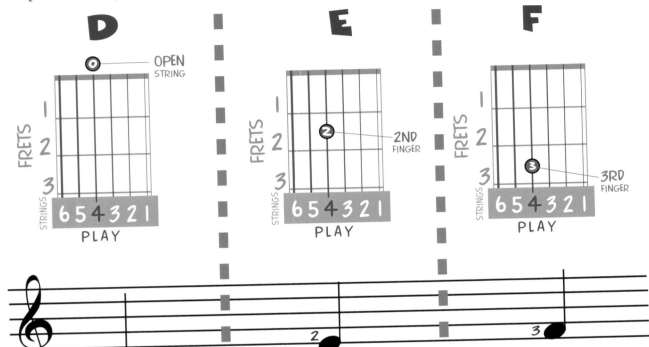

Here you will find notes on the 4th string. The nickname for D is **Down Below**. It is located down below the musical stave.

W is a **whole note** it's worth **4 beats**

count: D 2 3 4

H is a **Half note** it's worth **2 beats**

count: D 2 E 2

Q is a **Quarter note** only worth **1 beat**

count: D D D D

Maccy D had a festival.

Look at **lines 1** and **2** of the music. What do you notice?

The eighth note.

The **eighth** note is only worth **half a beat.** The **eighth** note is written like a **quarter note** but has a **small flag** attached to it.

$$\eighthnote = \frac{1}{8} \text{ note} = \frac{1}{2} \text{ a beat.}$$

If two or more eighth notes are written in **successive order**, they are attached by **one line**.

EXAMPLE:

could be written as ♫ or ♪♪♪♪ could be written as

The easiest way to **count eighth beats** are as follows: set the **tempo** with **quarter beats** on your **left hand** and with your **right hand** tap **coffee** beats.

Quarter notes you count as **"Tea"**.   Eighth notes you count as **"Coffee"**.

Tea   Tea   Tea   Tea   Cof-fee   Cof-fee   Cof-fee   Cof-fee

Try to **tap** this exercise with 2 hands at the same time. Play the **'Teas'** with your **left hand** and **'Coffees'** with the **right**.

CLAPPING RHYTHMS

Notes on the 4th string.

Peter's Exercise 1.

Peter's Exercise 2.

Peter's Exercise 3.

Peter's gone!

Spanish sliding surprise.

For this song you will learn the chord of **E Major.**
It is played a lot in many Spanish songs and when you
slide the chord into certain positions you will hear the
sound of Spain from your guitar.

¡ay caramba!

The positions being used in the song are **1st, 2nd** and **4th** on the **E chord.**

The position is indicated from your **fret** and **1st finger** position.

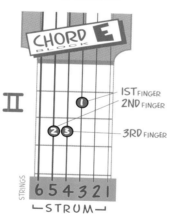

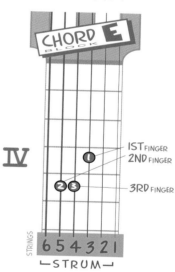

Remember when you slide a chord up the **fretboard** try to **hold the shape.** If you remove your fingers
from the strings you'll have to **rebuild** the **chord** each time.

Have a go at this chord exercise. **Remember** to hold the shape and **slide** the fingers.

| E | \ | \ | II | \ | \ | IV | \ | \ | II | \ | \ |
| E | \ | \ | IV | \ | \ | II | \ | \ | E | \ | \ |

floyd's weekend.
Slow Rock Ballad

This session we are going to look at **dynamics**.
Dynamics are added to pieces of music to give songs **phrasing** and **meaning**.

f	=	*forte*	=	**loud**
p	=	*piano*	=	*soft*
mf	=	*mezzo forte*	=	**moderately loud**
mp	=	*mezzo piano*	=	*moderately soft*
<	=	*(cresc) crescendo*	=	gradually **get louder**
>	=	*diminuendo*	=	**gradually** *get softer*

To help you **concentrate** on the dynamics with the **right hand** play the following workouts on **open strings.**

Workout 1.

Workout 2 (the echo).

Workout 3.

Workout 4.

Give it feel.

Notes on the 5th string.

Here you will find the notes on the **5th string**. Because the notes go below the musical stave we need extra lines. These are called **Ledger Lines**. Study through the exercises then have a go at 'Thumbs Up' on page 19. For this song we use only the **C** but it gives you more chance to practise 1/8th beats and reading some ledger line notes.

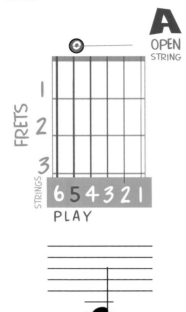

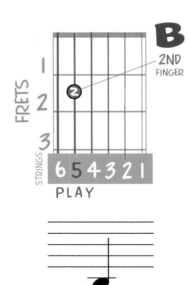

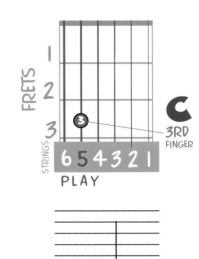

W is a **whole note** it's worth **4 beats**

Count: A 2 3 4

H is a **Half note** it's worth **2 beats**

Count: A 2 A 2

Q is a **Quarter note** only worth **1 beat**

Count: A   A   A   A

Thumbs up!

Scale of C major.

Here you will find the **C Major Scale.**
There are many different kinds of scales but
C Major Scale is known as the **Natural Scale.**

Southern strings.

It covers all notes from the **5th string** to the **1st**.

Notes on the 6th String.

Here you will find the notes on the **6th string**. You may notice how the finger numbers and fret numbers are exactly the same as the **first string.** This is because the first string is also called **E** and will mirror the same sound but at a higher pitch.

Have a go at **high E** and **low E** and hear the difference.

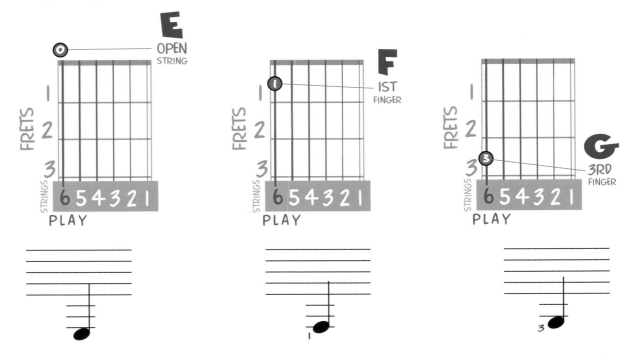

W is a **whole note** it's worth **4 beats**

Count: E 2 3 4

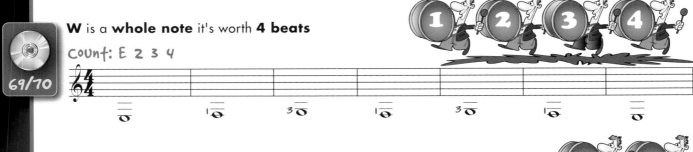

H is a **Half note** it's worth **2 beats**

Count: E 2 E 2

Q is a **Quarter note** only worth **1 beat**

Count: E E E E

Tapas @ 3.

fastest gun in the west.

Here we have a **new game** called **"Fastest gun in the West"**. Starting on the **open 6th string** play all the notes in the first position up to the first string. You should try to play all these notes in **under 5 seconds**. If you go under 5 seconds you will be the fastest gun in the west.

Time week 1: [   ] secs   **Time week 2:** [   ] secs

Three New chords...

Here you will find 3 new chords: **A, D & E7**.
The reason we play the **A chord** with fingers 2, 3 & 4 is so the finger behind can slide up and down for the D Triangle and **E7 chord**.

Remember the **first finger** never comes off the **3rd string** for this sequence.

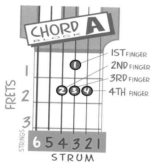

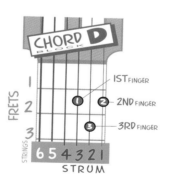

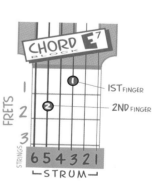

Boogie Woogie.

This is a new sign: `•/.` and this means repeat the previous bar.

| A \ \ \ | | •/. | | A \ \ \ | | •/. |
| D \ \ \ | | •/. | | A \ \ \ | | •/. |
| E7 \ \ \ | D \ \ \ | A \ \ \ | E7 E7 A ≀ ‖

The Tie.

The **Tie** is a **curved line** between **two notes** of the **same pitch**. The **first note is played** and the **second note is held** for however long the note is written. The first example is with open strings.

Count: E 2 3 Hold 2 3

Notice how, when the note has an **up stem**, the **tie** is written **below the notes.** When the note has a **down stem,** it is **written above.**

Dotted note fun.

In this workout we will look at **dotted quarter notes** (or **dotted crotchets**).
The **dot** after the note means add **half as much again** to the **length** of the note it's after.

EXAMPLES:

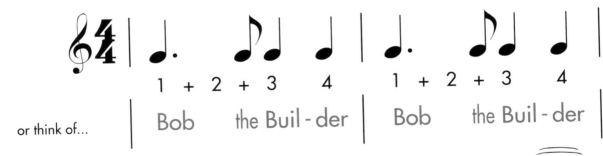

The **trickier** notes to count are the **1 beat notes** To break down this **rhythm** follow the chart below.

or think of... | Bob   the Buil - der | Bob   the Buil - der |

CLAPPING RHYTHMS

Workout 1

Workout 2

Workout 3

Scarborough Fair.

Are you going to Scarborough fair?
Parsley, sage, rosemary and thyme.
Remember me to one who lives there,
She once was a true love of mine.
She once was a true love of mine.

Sharps #.

Here you will find a new musical symbol called a **sharp**. A sharp increases a note by **one semitone** or on the guitar **one fret.**

Scale of A Harmonic Minor using G#.

Flats ♭.

The scale of **F major** has **one flat.** The flat is **B♭**. Notice how the **symbol** is **placed** on the **B line.**

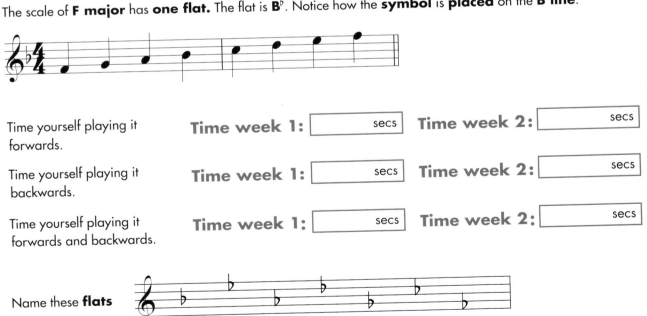

Time yourself playing it forwards.

Time week 1: [ ] secs **Time week 2:** [ ] secs

Time yourself playing it backwards.

Time week 1: [ ] secs **Time week 2:** [ ] secs

Time yourself playing it forwards and backwards.

Time week 1: [ ] secs **Time week 2:** [ ] secs

Name these **flats**

and put your **answers** in the **boxes.**

???

Scale of F Major using B♭.

Reggae Jam.

Don't worry too much, all this involves is **reading** and **playing** two notes at the **same time**.

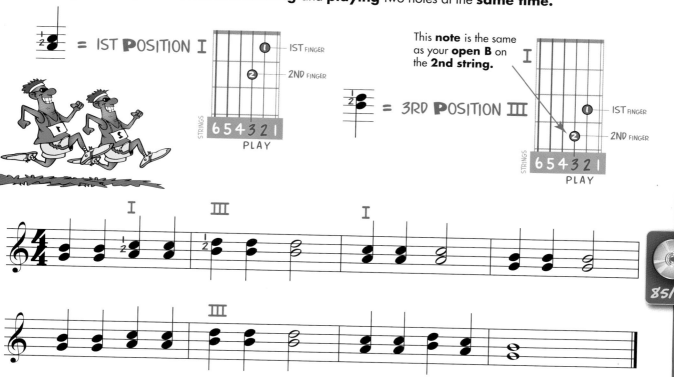

In **bar two** you may notice III written above. This means **3rd position.** If you take your **1st** and **2nd** finger on the **left hand** and **slide** them up to the **3rd** and **4th fret** you will be able to find **D & G.**

Right Hand.

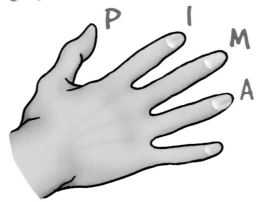

Here we will work on some **right hand picking** exercises. To make things easy we are going to start on **open strings**.

For this style of playing imagine each finger like a **digger** lifting a cable. This style of playing is known as **'Tirando'** which means **freestroke.**

Workout 1. Pluck away from the hole and do not use Restroke or Walking Fingers.

Workout 2.

This means '**repeat the previous bar**'.

License to thrill!

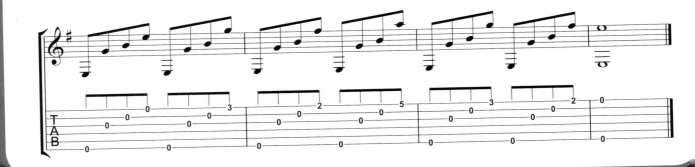

Blank staves.

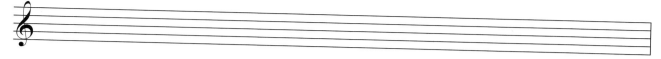

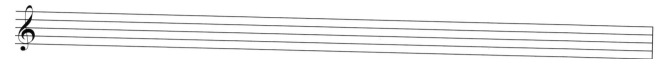

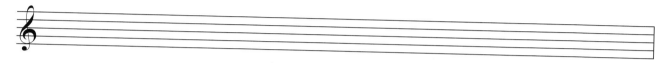

Blank Tab.

HARRY POTTER THEME

Blank chord blocks.

Blank staves.

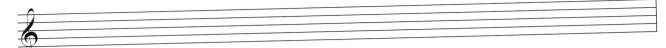

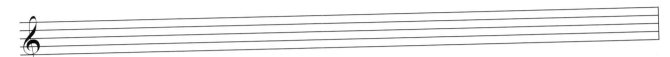

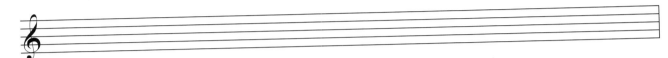

Blank Tab.

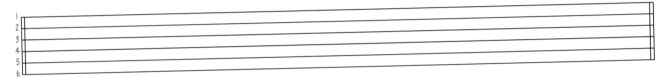

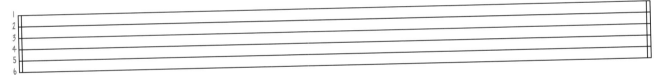

Blank chord blocks.

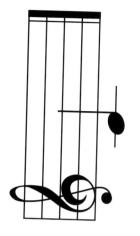

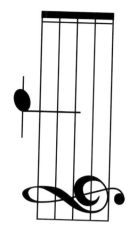

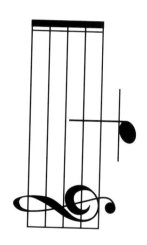

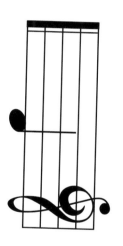

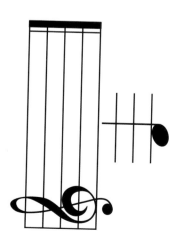

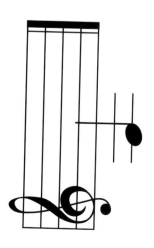

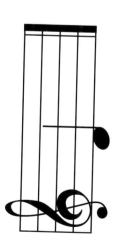

A = Aeroplane

C

G

G = Giant

B = Both ways

F

D = Down below

A

E

Congratulations.
You have now completed Guitar Trainer Book 2!

Guitar Trainer
BOOK 2

This is to certify that

_____
STUDENT NAME

has successfully completed

Guitar Trainer Book 2

_____
DATE ACCOMPLISHED

_____
AWARD ACHIEVED

_____
MEDAL PRESENTED

_____
COACH

_____
SIGNATURE OF COACH

THE
ROCK
& POP
FOUNDATION.
RAISING THE STANDARDS
IN MUSIC EDUCATION

THE STRUCTURE OF FERNS

Ferns belong to a division of the plant kingdom called Pteridophyta. *This name derives from the Greek words, 'pteris' – used in ancient times to describe a common fern, from 'petron' – a wing or a feather, and from 'phyton' meaning a plant. Although there is no one family to which ferns belong, they share many characteristics, making them easily distinguishable from most other plants.*

The properties common to all ferns include: their lack of flowers and seeds, and their distinctive method of reproduction; the creeping stems, or rhizomes; their leaves, called fronds, and their 'fiddle head' stage, and the occurrence of hair or scales on different parts of the plants.

Ferns may be broadly grouped according to their pattern of growth: there are crown-forming ferns, such as the Maidenhairs, whose fronds develop from a root ball or crown; ferns which develop no crown but have fronds growing directly from the rhizome, for example the Rabbit's-foot Fern; epiphytic ferns which are not parasites, although they attach themselves to trees or damp rocks and walls, for example the Stag's-horn Fern; and spleenworts which mostly belong to the genus Asplenium *(comprising over 700 species).*

Spores and reproduction

Unlike most garden plants, ferns produce neither flowers nor seeds which result in new plants. Instead, they develop *spores* which are minute, dust-like particles, produced, in their thousands, in spore holders called *sporangia*. The sporangia are usually found on the undersides or on the edges of the fronds, and are commonly clustered together (in groups of three or more), and then known as *sori*. Each group or sorus may be enclosed in a thin, protective cover called the *indusium* – an outgrowth of the epidermis – or, in the case of the Maidenhair ferns, a *false indusium* which is the rolled margin of the frond.

In some ferns, spores are found on certain 'fertile' fronds only, the non-spore-bearing ones being 'sterile'. This phenomenon is characteristic of the Royal Fern where spore-bearing fronds look quite different to the sterile ones, and are therefore referred to as *dimorphic*, that is, occurring in two forms.

When sporangia mature, they burst and scatter the fine spore dust, which is often carried by wind and water. If a spore falls on moist, favourable soil, it will germinate and develop into a heart-shaped plant – the *prothallus*. This leaf-like structure contains both the male and female reproductive organs, and, once fertilization has taken place, gives rise to the roots and fronds of a new fern. With the development of the fern, the prothallus withers and dies, and after about two years the new fern will begin to produce fertile fronds, with spores, to complete the reproductive cycle.

Rhizomes

The stems of ferns, from which the fronds and roots grow, are known as rhizomes. These are usually below the ground but may creep above it, as in the Rabbit's-foot Fern; they may climb – as in the climbing ferns (*Lygodium*); or may grow erect, like the Holly Fern. Tree ferns, on the other hand, have upright stems which are covered by the bases of old, but persistent, fronds; the erect stem is referred to as a *caudex*.

Fronds

Fern leaves, or fronds, emerge from the rhizomes or caudex. A frond is made up of a stalk or *stipe*, but where this meets the frond blade or *lamina*, it is known as the *rachis* (plural *rachids*). Branches from the rachis are called *secondary rachids*; the progression continues into tertiary rachids, and so on.

In nearly all ferns, fronds begin as *fiddle heads* or *croziers* – delicate curled up tips which unfold as they grow into the mature leaves. Fiddle heads are one of the distinguishing features of true ferns.

Scales and hair

Almost all ferns develop scales or hairs. These may be found on rhizomes, on the base of stipes, sometimes on the rachids and on the backs of fronds. The form that scales and hair may take varies between ferns and serves as a guide when identifying species.

Identifying ferns

Identifying ferns can be frustrating, as several ferns share many common features. There are, however, certain characteristics which can be used to facilitate the task: first, note the shape of the frond and the type of vein structure; then, observe whether scales or hair occur and if so, where; check the arrangement of sporangia – patterns may be fascinating and quite beautiful, but will vary between different fern plants – some occur on the leaf margins, some along the veins and others are just scattered on the backs of fronds. Another guide feature is the indusia or sporangia covers – and whether they occur at all; if they do, their shape can often help to identify a fern.

Taxonomists can also help laymen to identify ferns if they are provided with a good frond specimen containing sporangia; in the case of dimorphic plants, a sterile frond would also be required for identification purposes.

1 Early spring growth on a Common Tree Fern, showing the emerging fiddle heads which develop into lush, green foliage.
2 Characteristic hair is distinctly visible on the stipe, or stalk, of a developing frond.
3, 4 The variable arrangement of sporangia is evident on the frond of a Stag's-horn Fern (3) as compared to those on a Knysna Fern frond (4).

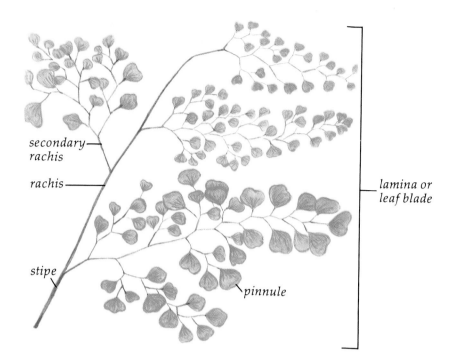

secondary rachis

rachis

stipe

lamina or leaf blade

pinnule

FROND FORMS

There are various frond shapes:

1 A fern leaf may be simple, or uncut, with a central vein bisecting a large lamina or leaf blade. This is characteristic of the Bird's-nest Fern, and of *Pyrrosia africana* which is endemic to the south-eastern parts of South Africa.

2 Some fronds are divided into *pinnae* (singular *pinna*): these are separate leaflets, each with a central vein and individually attached to the rachis. The fronds of the Sword Fern and the Button Fern represent the simplest type of *pinnate* frond.

3 Pinnae may be further divided into smaller segments or *pinnules*. This results in more delicate, lacy fronds, as seen in the Rabbit's-foot Fern.

4 In place of the pinnae, the rachis may support another type of leaf blade structure: one that is lobed. Even though lobes are divisions of the leaf blade, unlike pinnae, they are not divided into individual leaflets nor separately attached to the rachis. The Stag's-horn Fern and some *Polypodium* ferns have lobed or *pinnatifid* fronds.

1   2   3   4

GROWING FERNS INDOORS

Although not of the manic proportions that characterized Victorian England, the current interest in growing ferns is certainly increasing, and more and more people are turning to these decorative foliage plants to bring the fresh and restful touch of nature into their homes.

There are many places inside the home which could be made more attractive by the flowing grace of fern plants, but not all will be perfectly suited to the successful cultivation of each fern species. Some ferns are more tender than others and without the right conditions will not thrive at all, while others are happy with only their basic needs being satisfied. Sometimes, only trial and error will indicate the best position for a fern plant. However, the first step in raising healthy plants is to make sure that the following basic requirements are being met:

Light: Most ferns need good indirect light without the damaging heat of direct sunlight. Insufficient light will result in poor, spindly growth, while too much light could bleach foliage, and hot, direct sun would scorch it. A position near an east-facing window which gets a little of the early morning sun will suit many ferns, and most will thrive beside one that is north-facing, provided that any sun entering is filtered.

Air flow: Fern plants require a gentle flow of clean, free-circulating air, but dislike draughts from open doors or windows. Many do not like to be moved about from one location to another, so try to ensure that all the plant's requirements will be met before deciding upon a final location.

Soil: The soil used for potted ferns should contain plenty of humus and must be friable and well-drained. A healthy mixture can be made up using 7 parts good, sterilized garden soil, 3 parts granulated peat and 2 parts well-washed, coarse sand. To every 2 plastic buckets (10 ℓ) of this mixture, add 60 g of bone phosphate and 2 cups of pea-sized charcoal. The charcoal will help to keep the soil sweet.

Watering: Ferns must never be allowed to dry out completely. The soil should be kept evenly moist so that the plant's roots are kept damp, but saturation of the soil mixture must be avoided.

Many ferns originate in tropical areas where humidity levels are high, so indoor ferns will need extra care, especially where a dry atmosphere has been caused by heating or air-conditioning systems. An effective way of increasing humidity indoors is to place the container on a layer of pebbles in a shallow dish or drip-tray. Pour some water into the dish until it reaches a level just below the top of the pebbles (the pot itself must never stand in water). Provided that you frequently replenish the water in the dish, the plant's humidity requirements will be satisfied. Another way of ensuring higher humidity is by grouping plants together: this creates a micro-climate, and water transpired by the leaves, is reabsorbed by the massed canopy of foliage before it has a chance to evaporate.

Feeding: Ferns do not require extensive feeding, although occasional applications will encourage lush foliage. It is advisable to use organic fertilizers, such as SM3 Seaweed Extract, Farmura Organic Fertilizer or Maxicrop liquid seaweed, at half strength; and feeding is best done in spring or midsummer. A top dressing of leaf soil, added in the spring months, is also beneficial. Before adding a fertilizer, always make sure that the soil is damp; apply the mixture or solution around the inside rim of the pot, without touching any of the foliage.

If a plant is not thriving, don't immediately conclude that it can be revived with fertilizers. Rather, try to determine the reason for its affected state – the answer may well lie in poor ventilation, over- or under-watering, insufficient light or inadvertent exposure to strong sunlight, or to insect pests.

Selecting and displaying indoor plants

There are many ferns that grow well indoors and many ways in which to display the plants. Those most suited to indoor cultivation include Maidenhair ferns, Bird's-nest and Mother ferns, the Holly Fern, Rabbit's-foot Fern, the Hand Fern, the Sword Fern, the Boston Fern and its cultivars (*Nephrolepis* species), the Button Fern, Golden Fern, Stag's-horn, the Shield ferns (*Polystichum* species), Ribbon Fern and the Table Fern.

After selecting the fern you want to grow, the next step is to choose a container and manner of display. There is a wide range of containers available, from fairly small terracotta, ceramic and plastic pots to large tubs – diverse in colour, shape and material. Potted ferns can form decorative displays on table tops, ledges and on bookshelves. They also blend well with other foliage and flowering plants, their

ften graceful and delicate fronds bringing natural softness to an arrangement. Some of the larger-growing ferns, such as the Bird's-nest, can have a dramatic impact when displayed separately in a corner pot or against a plain background.

anging Baskets Baskets of ferns are extremely attractive in any oom, hallway or at the entrance of the house. Modern plastic varieties are available which have their own drip trays attached, but the ost suitable basket for ferns should be at least 30-45 cm in diameter nd made of heavy-gauge wire. To prepare the basket, place it in a ucket or up-turned pot to keep it steady; line the inside with a thick ayer of living sphagnum moss (green) and then with a sheet of black lastic with holes punched in the bottom. Then add a layer of soil (see bove for soil mixture), which should be mixed with a quantity of ydrostock so as to increase its water-holding capacity. Place the fern n the basket and fill it with soil, firming it *lightly* around the plant. efore suspending the fern plant, immerse the basket in water to enure that the soil is thoroughly moistened. Ferns well-suited to hangng include the popular Maidenhairs, the Boston Fern and its cultiars, and the Rabbit's-foot Fern.

errariums Some of the more tender ferns will grow well in terrarums, where moisture levels are constantly high and where effective rotection from draughts and dry heat can be ensured. The following erns make particularly attractive displays behind the glass: *Adiantum addianum microphyllum*, small specimens of the Bird's-nest plant, the ibbon Fern, *Marsilea* species and the Hand Fern.

A terrarium planted with a young Bird's-nest and a Maidenhair Fern.
A Ribbon Fern and Blechnum gibbum, *both in cork containers, form an attractive display against the Oregon pine table surface.*
, 5 Hanging baskets of various Sword ferns contribute freshness and colour to both a cooking (3) and a living (5) area.
A magnificent specimen of the Boston Fern displays the vitality of nature, enhanced by the carved wooden chest on which it stands.

4

5

5

GROWING FERNS OUTDOORS

For gardeners who have problems growing plants successfully in the shady areas of their gardens, ferns provide an immediate solution, allowing for the usually stark shaded parts to be converted into beautiful woodland scenes. Ferns will flourish beneath the shady cover of large trees, although it is not wise to plant them under dense evergreens where they would have to compete with the trees' roots for essential moisture and nutrients. Planted on the perimeter of a tree group, however, they will receive dappled shade and perhaps a little of the early morning or late afternoon sun which will suit their growth needs perfectly. Some ferns have adapted to shaded, rocky slopes where no other growth seems possible.

1

Planting possibilities

Apart from providing a solution to the problematic areas, however, ferns will fit well into any garden space, forming ideal background plantings, lining bare walls and fences, and blending with flowers in rockeries and garden beds.

In mild frost-free areas, many ferns can be planted on the south side of the house but, because these plants have adapted to forest environments, in most other areas it is best to choose a site that will satisfy their shade-loving natures.

The shaded areas of the garden are also the ones most likely to retain moisture longer, and this, too, will suit these plants. Because of their need for moisture, it is often wise to plant ferns in low-lying parts of the garden, or on gently sloping ground which would ensure good drainage. *Shaded* fish ponds and garden pools are ideal locations for ferns – not only will their attractive foliage enhance the setting, but their roots will be certain to receive constant moisture here.

Tree Ferns make striking features in larger gardens but cannot be grown in cool temperate climates and careful attention should be given to their cultural requirements. The epiphytic ferns, such as the Stag's-horn, are impressive plants with an interesting pattern of development. They do not grow independently but will grow well on rotting wood stumps or on damp rocky walls in tropical areas.

An alternative to planting ferns in garden beds is the decorative outdoor display of potted ferns. These can be attractively grouped

2

3

4

with other plants of contrasting size and foliage, and placed in bare corners, around paved areas or against walls and fences. In patio areas, ferns can be arranged among other plants or suspended from hanging baskets, where their bright foliage will cascade gracefully over the container's sides.

Soil preparation

Before preparing a fern bed, make sure that the soil drains freely, as ferns will not thrive in ground that is prone to waterlogging during wet weather. Dig the ground over deeply and add plenty of sifted compost and/or imported peat with a dressing of bone phosphate at the rate of 60 g per square metre. Work the soil up into a fine tilth, level with a rake and water well so as to settle the soil.

Once you have planted the ferns, allow water from a hose to run gently over the soil surface until you are sure that the bed is wet but not sodden. Further waterings should be lighter, but sufficient to ensure that the soil remains moist.

Careful attention should be given to the growth patterns of the ferns you are planting: tall plants should be set towards the back of a bed and shorter varieties in front. Also, remember to allow plenty of space when planting ferns such as the Rabbit's-foot, which has a spreading pattern of growth.

Care should also be taken to plant ferns out of the reach of damaging winds. The following locations would all afford some degree of protection from the wind: the base of a slope, in beds among hardier plants, beneath a tree, close to the house or garden wall and also on sheltered patios.

Selecting garden and patio ferns

When buying a fern from a nursery, choose one that is healthy-looking – free from blemishes and pests. The state of the foliage is always a good indicator of a plant's condition and should never be pale in colour or sparse for that species. The ferns most suitable for outdoor growth include: some of the Maidenhair Ferns, Holly Fern, Tree ferns, Rabbit's-foot Fern and Royal Fern for cool temperate areas; for other areas try also Mother Fern, Sword Fern, Stag's-horn Fern, Hand Fern, Button Fern and many of the *Blechnum* species.

1   An old picnic hamper provides a novel alternative for displaying Sword ferns on a patio.
2   Some ferns, such as this Pteris vittara, *can be grown in the most awkward spots, where plant growth would otherwise seem impossible.*
3   *A lush* Pteris *fern arches gracefully over the shaded pond – a location where essential moisture is ensured.*
4   *The Common Maidenhair Fern, well-suited to outdoor container cultivation, has clearly benefitted from its sheltered position close to the house and from the dappled sunlight which it receives.*
5   *Versatile* Nephrolepis *ferns serve as a decorative foliage border to this paved entrance.*
6   Dicksonia antartica, *with the beautiful colour-contrasting foliage of young and mature fronds, forms a graceful and impressive centre-piece in this mixed bed.*

5

6

7

PROPAGATION OF FERNS

There are several methods by which to raise new ferns. These can be summarized into, first, vegetative propagation and, second, propagation from spores.

Vegetative propagation

This kind of propagation can be undertaken in four different ways: by the division of crowns, of rhizomes, of stolons, and from bulblets.

Division of crowns Plants which develop crowns, such as the Maidenhair ferns and *Pteris* species lend themselves to division at these points. Ferns with only one crown should not be divided in this way, but those which develop more than one crown allow for easy separation. Use either a sharp knife or the gentle force of the hands. Division is best undertaken in spring when new growth is on its way, or when many plants may well have outgrown their pots.

Take great care when handling and dividing ferns not to damage any part of the crown of the existing plant. Once divided, plant each section in a clean pot with a layer of drainage material (small pebbles or stone chips). Set the new division at the same depth as it was growing before and fill the pot in with soil, firming it *lightly* around the new plant. Water well. Discoloured fronds should be cut off, but at least a third of the green leaves should be left to continue the process of photosynthesis.

Division of rhizomes Ferns which have creeping rhizomes (either above or below the ground) offer an easy method of propagation. Those with underground stems must be dug up: using a sharp knife, cut as many sections of a rhizome as required, making sure that each one contains new frond growth. Plant the cut end about 3 cm below the surface of a suitable, moist soil mixture, allowing the growing point to rest on the surface. In order to avoid movement until the new roots are established, peg the cutting down to the soil surface.

For ferns with rhizomes that creep above the ground, it is more advisable to encourage the development of a new plant before severing it from its parent: select a rhizome that has at least one growing point and anchor it to the ground at a point near the growing tip, just behind a frond. In time the pegged down section of the rhizome will develop roots, and when this happens, the rhizome can be severed from the main plant and potted up.

Propagation from stolons All of the *Nephrolepis* ferns send out fine stolons that creep along the soil surface. If these stolons are pegged down in a well-prepared soil, they will eventually root themselves and can, at this stage, be cut from the parent plant and potted up. This genus of fern can also be propagated by division of the crowns.

Propagation from bulblets Some plants, the Mother Fern for instance, develop tiny bulblets on the upper surface of their fronds which grow into miniature fern plants. Simply detach the bulblets from the fronds and plant them in trays filled with a suitable potting mixture. High levels of humidity are favoured for successful development, and can be provided by covering the pots with glass or plastic until the bulblets have rooted. The trays should be uncovered at a gradual rate so as to allow the little plants to adapt to the less humid conditions outside the plastic or glass cover.

Propagation from spores

This method of propagation demands perseverance, delicate handling and special care, but it is most rewarding to witness the eventual development of the tiny fern after the long wait, which can be up to a year.

Spores must be *ripe* before they can be gathered: at this stage, the sporangia on mature fronds will take on a dark brown colour and, if examined under a magnifying glass, will have a frayed look, as if ready to burst. Cut off a frond, or part thereof, which contains plenty of sporangia and place this on a sheet of paper. The spores will start emerging from their cases almost immediately, and soon the paper will be covered with what looks like a fine dust. Fold the paper and store it in a safe place.

Make up a mixture of 2 parts granulated peat, 2 parts clean, fairly coarse sand and 1 part sterilized soil; sift this through a 12 mm sieve and then boil (using a pressure cooker is ideal) the soil mixture to make sure that it is clean. The pans in which the spores are to be sown must also be *thoroughly* clean. This can be achieved by washing them in a solution of 1 part household bleach to 9 parts water; thereafter rinse well in boiled water and allow to dry. Place a 12 mm layer of fine, sterilized gravel at the bottom of the pan and cover this with 2,5 cm of the prepared soil; level off and moisten from the bottom with boiled water; allow to drain.

Taking a small quantity of the spores on the tip of a knife, mix with finely sifted sterilized sand and scatter this evenly over the surface of the soil. Cover the pan with glass, or enclose it in a plastic bag, which should be inflated and securely tied at the top. Plastic containers with lids can be used instead of pans, but these too must be sterilized before sowing the spores. If the pan has been covered with glass it may, at times, require watering. This should be done from the bottom, using boiled water that has cooled. Keep the pan in a bright position but out of direct sunlight, at a temperature of between 20 °C and 26 °C.

There is an easier way for the not so experienced gardener to raise some of the smaller ferns from spores: place a potted fern on a layer of sifted sand, mixed with peat and a small quantity of pea-sized charcoal, in a large, plastic drip tray. In a very still atmosphere, the spores will drift down on to the sand mixture and, if this is kept moist and the pot is placed in a warm, well-lit spot, they will germinate.

The rate of germination varies between fern plants and according to local conditions, but after some time a green filament will appear on the surface of the soil. Examined under a magnifying glass, a series of minute chain-like cells are visible. These

cells divide and produce a heart-shaped structure: the *prothallus*, or gametophyte. During the ensuing weeks, both the male and the female reproductive structures will develop on different areas of the prothallus. From this point on, it is *extremely important* that the soil be kept really moist as the male sperm will require water in which to swim towards and fertilize the female egg cell. Once fertilized, the egg, drawing nourishment from the prothallus, will develop into a minute frond. It is only after about five months to a year that secondary fronds will appear above the ground, that the rhizome will develop and that the prothallus will shrivel and disappear. After about two years of growth, the new fern will begin to produce spore-bearing fronds.

1   *Young fern plants, seen growing from the dark bulblets at the tips of the fronds on a Mother Fern, can be carefully detached and potted up to produce a new plant.*
2   *Dark-brown sporangia, or spore covers, burst to release the ripe, dust-like spores, each of which represents a potential fern.*
3   *The creeping rhizomes of* Davallia fejeensis *lend themselves to further propagation by division (5).*
4   *The heart-shaped* prothallus, *containing both male and female reproductive organs, is shown in different stages of development (right to left), from its earliest stage to the appearance of the first leaflets and roots of a new Maidenhair Fern.*
5   *A rhizome, containing new growth, is pegged down to the surface of the potting mixture. It will be severed from the main plant once its own roots develop.*

2

3

4

5

YEAR ROUND CARE OF FERNS

Once established, most ferns require routine attention. There are a few basic procedures which, carried out in different seasons, will ensure the general health of your home-cultivated ferns.

Spring

This is the time to take a close look at your ferns, to examine size and growth, to repot where necessary and, if so desired, to divide plants for further propagation.

At about the beginning of early spring, potted ferns should be neatened up by removing any old fronds, but take care not to damage any emerging fiddle heads (new fronds) in the process. A little of the surface soil should be scratched away and replaced with sifted compost. The old fronds of garden plants must also be removed, as well as those that have fallen. The ground outside should be mulched with sifted compost, taking care not to cover any rhizomes which grow above the ground, as in the case of the Rabbit's-foot Fern.

Both indoor and garden ferns will benefit from an application of half-diluted organic fertilizer, but avoid touching the crowns of the plants with any of the solution. Water lightly after applying.

Repotting ferns Any ferns which are pot-bound or which have outgrown their containers should be repotted. Pot-bound plants are those whose roots have exhausted the soil and dominated the available space within the container. To test for this, turn the pot upside down and tap the rim against a table; this will enable the plant to emerge quite easily. If there is little or no soil and only a root ball, repotting into a larger container is necessary. If the roots of a plant are growing through the base of a pot, this also signals the need for transplanting the fern into a bigger container.

A fern should be transferred to a pot that is only one size larger, unless it is a vigorous grower, in which case it can be transplanted into one that is two sizes bigger. New pots must be thoroughly clean and should contain adequate drainage holes.

Cover the base of the pot with a layer of drainage material (small pebbles, stone chips), then add a layer of potting soil (see page 4). Before turning the plant out of its original pot, make sure that the soil is well moistened so that most of the existing soil remains around the root clump. Small plants will emerge easily if they are turned upside down and the rim is tapped against a table; with larger specimens it may be necessary to wrap a piece of cloth around the pot and then to tap it with a wooden mallet. Place the fern in its new pot at the same depth as it was in its previous container; fill in with soil and firm *lightly* (ferns do not like being firmed in too hard). Water well and place in a shady position.

Division If a plant becomes too large for convenient container growth, it is best to divide it, and early spring is the time to perform this task. Cut off some of the plant's fronds, leaving a few to ensure continued photosynthesis once the division has been carried out. Plant the divisions in the same manner as you would repot, again making sure that the new sections are planted at the same depth as they were previously growing. If you are dividing a fern whose rhizomes grow on top of the soil (*Davallia*, for example), be certain that the new divisions are replanted above the soil, and pegged down. Once planted, fern divisions should be watered with a fine spray.

Summer

The most important factors in summer are moisture and pest control. During hot, dry weather, potted soil and garden beds should be kept moist at all times. It is a good idea to mist the plants regularly and to set up pebble trays if conditions become very dry or as humidity levels drop. Tree ferns require extra care during dry periods – be sure that their soil is always moist and spray the stems frequently. All other outdoor ferns should be watered at about mid-morning.

In mid-summer, apply liquid fertilizers, at half strength, to all ferns – potted or in the garden. During the summer months plants should be checked regularly for pests and diseases, and must be treated promptly should these arise.

Autumn

Fern growth will start to slow down as autumn approaches, and the plants will require a little less water as the days get cooler.

Do not make the mistake of cutting off old fronds from deciduous ferns in the autumn, as these serve as a protection for the plant's roots. In the colder parts of the country, a good mulching of the ground will also assist in protecting the roots from frost and cold conditions. Where ferns are grown under deciduous trees, remove any leaves which fall, as these may smother the fern plants.

Winter

Ferns require minimal care during the winter months. It is best to keep the soil on the 'dry side of moist', taking care, however, not to let it dry out.

Pests and diseases

Several different insect pests may be attracted to your ferns. Your best defence against them is the careful and regular inspection of the plants (for example, each time you water them) so that any occurrence can be dealt with as soon as possible.

Ants Although ants do not actually harm ferns, they do encourage the incidence of other pests such as aphids and scale. The area in which ferns are growing must be kept clear of ants – try to locate (and destroy) their nest, rather than spray them near the plants as sprays may be harmful to the ferns themselves.

Aphids These small sucking insects – generally green in colour – are most troublesome during spring. They are particularly attracted to the delicate fiddle heads, sucking the juice and destroying them before they can mature. Small infestations can be dealt with by spraying the plant with a jet of plain or soapy water. Bad attacks should be controlled with Bio Sprayday (active ingredient permethrin).

Eelworms or nematodes These are microscopic pests which attack the roots, and sometimes the stems, of plants. They are unlikely to be a problem if soil is sterilized before planting, as they usually enter the root system from infected soil. Should a fern appear to be suffering without any obvious or detectable cause, it would be wise to turn the plant out of its pot and to examine the roots. If nodules are visible, it is best to destroy the plant and to discard the infected soil. Fern earthworms are minute worm-like creatures which can only be seen clearly with a microscope, and should not be mistaken for a larger species which is just visible to the naked eye and which is harmless, living in plant material which is already decaying.

Mealy Bugs These bugs have the appearance of tiny tufts of cotton

3

4

5

6

7

wool with two long threads protruding from their backs. They usually collect around the bases of the fronds and can have a very damaging effect. If the infestation is light, mealy bugs can be removed with a cotton bud which has been dipped into a 50:50 solution of methylated spirits and water. However, at a more serious stage of invasion, it would be better to discard the plant and start afresh. Make sure that any plants nearby are not also infested.

Slugs and snails These pests come out at night and may eat the foliage of ferns in greenhouses and in garden beds. Snail bait, placed on the shelves in the greenhouse or on saucers, can be used to control the attacks, but these creatures can also be trapped by laying grapefruit skins or cabbage leaves, smeared with dripping, among the plants at night. These will attract the pests, which should be collected and destroyed the following morning.

Scale Soft brown scale is the kind most likely to attack fern plants. These small, brown pests have an oval form and congregate on the rachids (stems) and along the midribs of the fronds. Mild infestations can be controlled by wiping the insects off with a cotton bud, dipped into a mixture of methylated spirits and water in equal parts. Try to keep the area free of ants which encourage these pests, and check plants regularly to ensure that scale does not return.

White fly These minute white flying insects settle on the undersides of fern fronds and suck the sap. They can become very troublesome if they are not treated at an early stage. Control by spraying with Bio Sprayday (active ingredient permethrin). Before using these pesticides, however, it is advisable to test their effect on one frond first. If the leaf is not harmed in any way, it is safe to spray the whole plant, paying particular attention to the undersides of the fronds. If ferns are grown in a greenhouse, be careful to protect other plants, especially fuchsias, from white fly attacks.

Woodlice Some ferns are prone to attacks by woodlice, which eat the fronds. They are small, grey crustaceans with numerous legs and usually collect under stones and other objects on the ground. Attacks can be avoided by keeping the ground around the fern beds clear of debris. Should the pests be spotted, however, spray them *on the ground* with Malathion Greenfly Killer (active ingredient malathion) but do not allow any part of the fern to be touched with the spray.

Diseases

Few diseases will attack the fern which is properly nurtured and cared for. Should one occur, however, it is likely to be 'brown leaf'. This results in the development of brown, elongated patches on the fronds, giving the plant a blighted appearance and causing fronds to die prematurely. Cut off the affected fronds, and if the problem persists spray the plant with a dilute solution of Bordeaux Mixture or other remedy containing copper sulphate as the active ingredient.

Note: The application of pesticides or other chemical controls should be undertaken with care, as fern plants tend to be sensitive to the chemical ingredients.

1, 2 *A Maidenhair Fern, which has outgrown its pot (1) is divided, trimmed and repotted (2) into a larger container.*
3, 4 *A Pteris fern (3) is neatened up (4) in spring, by cutting away all dead and dying foliage.*
5 *Slug damage on a Bird's-nest Fern.*
6 *Mealy bug on a Shield Fern.*
7 *Brown scale clustered on the rachis of a Bird's-nest Fern.*

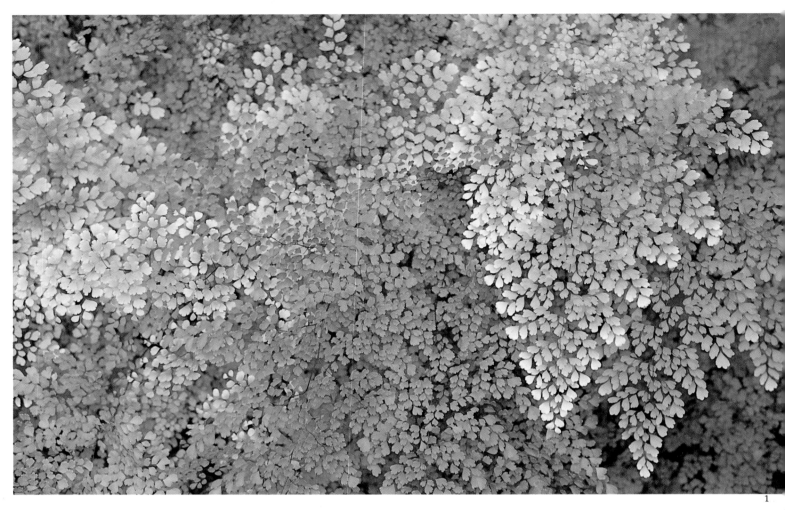

1

SOME COMMON FERNS

Ferns are the most beautiful of all non-flowering plants, and many of them are also very adaptable to conditions in our homes and gardens, even though they are far from their natural habitats. The species listed below are usually available from nurseries by mail-order and from garden centres; the widest range of ferns can be obtained from specialist nurseries.

ADIANTUM

This large genus comprises some 200 species, known collectively as the Maidenhair ferns. The plants vary widely in their appearance and characteristics, but all have an appealingly delicate, airy foliage. Most species require a high level of humidity and bright, indirect light and prefer acid soil. An ideal soil composition can be made by mixing leaf-mould and coarse sand in equal parts, together with a little bone-meal.

Many *Adiantum* species thrive especially well when they are slightly pot-bound.

Propagation: most species can be easily grown from spores, or by division during the initial spring growing period. Plant the divisions 30 cm to 60 cm apart.

2

Adiantum capillus-veneris
Common Maidenhair

This is the best-known of all the species within the genus, and is distributed world-wide. It is surrounded by many legends: according to a German one, the plant originated when a beautiful maiden plunged over a cliff when her lover turned into a wolf, and at the place where she fell, a spring appeared and her hair became a spreading fern.

Common Maidenhair has a short rhizome which gives rise to upright fronds. Pinnae are wedge-shaped and are carried on wiry, black rachids (the midribs of the fronds). The pinnae of the cultivar 'Brilliantelse' are more thickly packed on the rachids, and the plant has a compact habit of growth, which makes it an attractive pot fern.

3

The 'Fragrance' cultivar, on the other hand, has a more open growth pattern, with the pinnae widely distributed on long rachids. A large, well-developed plant makes a very decorative indoor display.

Outdoors, the Common Maidenhair plant thrives in a position of light shade.

Adiantum hispidulum/A. pubescens
Rosy Maidenhair

This species comes from the Old World tropics and, in appearance, is not a typical Maidenhair. The fronds are almost palmate in shape, usually about 20 cm in length and form dense clumps; pinnae are rhombic-oblong and borne on long, branching rachids. The leaf buds and young leaflets are a rosy pink (which gives the plant its common name), turning to green as the fern matures. Rosy Maidenhair needs a lower level of humidity than most other members of the genus.

Adiantum poirettii

This species occurs in most parts of the world. In South Africa, it is distributed from the Cape through the eastern parts of the country to the northern borders. Its favoured habitat is wet and shaded.

This fern has a slender, creeping rhizome which is covered in small, brown scales. Fronds are closely-spaced and arching and individual pinnae are fan-shaped. The thin stipe is black or dark-brown and up to 25 cm in length. *A. poirettii* is an attractive species, which can be grown in the garden as well as indoors; it is rarely available in the UK.

Adiantum raddianum/A. cuneatum
Fritz Luthii

Indigenous to Brazil, this fern's pinnae are wedge-shaped and a little coarse. Although vulnerable to frost, it is an especially easy Maidenhair to cultivate, and is very popular as an indoor plant. Propagation is from spores which, under favourable growing conditions, rapidly form fern colonies. The plant has a short, slender, creeping rhizome, and erect, stiff, evergreen fronds growing to between 25 cm and 45 cm in length. The stipe can grow up to 30 cm long.

1 Common Maidenhair
2 Clusters of sporangia, containing spores, develop on the margins of the fronds on the Common Maidenhair Fern
3 Rosy Maidenhair
4 *Adiantum poirettii*
5 Fritz Luthii

ASPLENIUM

This genus encompasses a full 700 species and more, varying widely in both appearance and characteristics. They are collectively and universally known as spleenworts, a name that originated in Scotland, where the plants once provided the essence of a tea infusion taken as a tonic.

Asplenium ferns grow from a single crown and are many-fronded to produce a fountain-like effect. The fronds may be either narrow or broad, depending on the particular species, but all spleenworts share a common spore arrangement: the indusia, or sporangia covers, are always long and narrow and develop along (and are linked to) the principal vein structure of the frond on which they appear.

As a general rule, the *Asplenium* plants need well-drained soil containing leaf-mould; and plenty of warmth, shade and moisture.

Asplenium bulbiferum
Mother Fern

The Mother Fern, indigenous to Australia, New Zealand and India, can under ideal conditions grow into a large plant. It has feathery, arching fronds which, indoors, grow to 30 cm or more in length and up to 23 cm wide. The sterile fronds are broader than the spore-bearing ones of the mature specimens – these distinctively different shapes making it an especially interesting plant. The tiny bulblets that form on the upper surface of the fronds develop into miniature plants which, with care, can be detached and potted up.

The Mother Fern can be grown out of doors in deep shade and a minimum temperature of 10° C. Indoors, it prefers a low level of indirect light and relatively high levels of humidity. The soil for this fern should be kept consistently moist but never soggy.
Propagation: from spores, by stem division or from bulblets.

Asplenium lunulatum

This species, which has no common name, is found in the south and eastern coastal regions of South Africa and, sparsely scattered, farther north in Zimbabwe and Malawi. Its natural habitat is the deeply shaded and moist forest floor.

A. lunulatum has a short, prostrate rhizome that is covered with brown scales. Its fronds are long and look a little like those of the sword fern. It is a useful plant for the damp, shady parts of the garden, but in a cool temperate climate should only be grown indoors in medium, indirect light. This fern plant requires a well-drained soil which should never be allowed to become waterlogged. *A. lunulatum* may not always be readily available in all parts of the country.
Propagation: from spores; and plantlets, formed on the rachis of mature fronds, can be persuaded to root into a suitable soil mix.

Asplenium nidus
Bird's-nest Fern

Indigenous to tropical Asia and Polynesia, the Bird's-nest Fern has beautiful, broad, undivided, glossy, light-green leaves with wavy margins. The tongue-like fronds rise from the crown, forming a bird's-nest shape, and as new centre leaves unfold, the older ones gradually die off.

This fern is popular as an indoor plant where its height rarely exceeds about 30 cm, but given extra warmth and humidity, it can grow as high as 120 cm. The plant dislikes being moved around, and needs to be kept out of cold draughts, especially in winter. Indirect, low-level light is preferred, and the fern will thrive in humid conditions. In summer when the weather is hot and dry, it should be placed on a pebble tray to increase atmospheric moisture. Feed with organic fertilizer once a month during summer. If grown in a greenhouse, the Bird's-nest Fern should be well protected from snails and wood-lice.
Propagation: from spores.

1 Mother Fern
2 *Asplenium lunulatum*
3 Bird's-nest Fern

3

'PSEUDO' OR FALSE FERNS

There is a group of plants, indigenous to South Africa, all of which are frequently mistaken for ferns. These plants, commonly referred to as the Asparagus Ferns, are in fact members of the lily family (*Liliaceae*).

Protasparagus densiflorus 'Sprengeri' (previously *Asparagus densiflorus* 'Sprengeri') produces outwardly curving stems, up to 60 cm long, with bright-green, needle-like leaves. A mature plant may, under favourable conditions, produce tiny flowers and later berries, which bear witness to the fact that the plant is not a true fern.

Protasparagus densiflorus 'Myersii' (previously *Asparagus densiflorus* 'Myersii') also develops rich green, needle-like leaves, between 30 cm and 60 cm long, but these are more densely assembled along the stems, and have a soft, bushy appearance which gives rise to the common names 'Cats' Tails' or 'Foxtails'.

Protasparagus setaceus (previously *Asparagus plumosus*) bears fine, lacy leaf growth which is flat and splayed rather than arching. The leaves are arranged on wiry stems with sharp prickles. Under ideal conditions, the plant may develop tiny white flowers and then berries. This plant is used by florists as a backing for bouquets or in buttonholes.

Protasparagus densiflorus 'Myersii'

Protasparagus densiflorus 'Sprengeri'

Protasparagus setaceus

15

BLECHNUM

One of the more extensive of the fern genera, *Blechnum* comprises some 200 species, most of them indigenous to the tropical regions of the southern hemisphere. Fronds can be upright or pendant, and in hardier species are usually a darker green than in the softer ones. The infertile pinnae of the *Blechnums* are normally wider than those which are fertile.

These ferns are suitable for indoor growth and, in warm or tropical climates, make attractive garden displays.

Blechnum australe

Widely distributed from the Cape and the eastern parts of South Africa to Kenya in the north, this fern is also found on Tristan da Cunha and Gough Island. In South Africa, it grows on the shaded banks of streams and near waterfalls, and is good for tropical gardens where it prefers shady, damp places. It will, however, grow in full sun under which conditions its fronds will be smaller, but also tougher. Indoors, the plant grows best in a medium to bright light. Moisture is a priority requirement in all situations.

The stem of this plant is prostrate and covered with brown scales. Fronds are sword-shaped and grow to a length of between 25 cm and 30 cm; the new fronds are usually pink in colour.
Propagation: by division or from spores (fertile fronds are generally produced once a year).

Blechnum gibbum/Lomaria gibba

This species is an attractive, dwarf tree fern with a crown of loosely spreading fronds. The trunk, or stipe, grows to between 90 cm and 150 cm tall, and gives rise to frond stalks and massed aerial roots.

B. gibbum needs a consistently moist, fairly acid soil and, outdoors (in tropical and sub-tropical gardens) prefers a position which has light to open shade. Being a fairly hardy plant, however, it will tolerate drier soils, and will also withstand short periods of direct sunlight, but will then require good watering. Indoors, it enjoys bright indirect light or, at most, curtain-filtered sunlight.
Propagation: from spores.

Blechnum tabulare/Lomaria boryana
Mountain Blechnum

Originally from the cold and windy southern islands of Tierra del Fuego and the Falklands, Mountain Blechnum is also found in South Africa's Cape Province and in the eastern regions of that country, in the Malagasy Republic and as far north as Tanzania. It is one of the most striking-looking members of the genus – an evergreen with glossy, deep-green leaves that arch elegantly. At an advanced age, the plant develops a caudex of up to a metre tall and from 7,5 cm to 15 cm in diameter, giving it the appearance of a small tree-fern.

Mountain Blechnum makes an attractive outdoor feature, where it prefers deep shade and a moist, fairly acid soil. Indoors, it thrives in low-level, indirect light (for instance, close to a south-facing window in the southern hemisphere, and north-facing in the northern). Ideal temperatures are 10° C to 15° C at night and between 21° C and 26° C during the day. Fairly high humidity levels are required.
Propagation: from spores or, preferably, by division in spring, at the start of the growing period, in order to give the plant an entire season to establish itself.

1

2

3

16

CYATHEA

The largest of the tree-fern groups – comprising more than 350 individual plants – *Cyathea* ferns are indigenous to the tropics (where the species usually have spiny trunks) and to the subtropical regions (where most of the species are spineless). The thick, upright trunk is clothed with a tangle of aerial roots and with the bases of dead fronds which, together, combine to create a fibrous, moisture-retaining covering. The fronds are usually large, and spread outwards. Most species are easily grown provided they are not subjected to temperature extremes.

Cyathea australis/Alsophila australis
Australian Tree Fern; Rough Tree Fern

This is a magnificent species, which can grow to almost 7 metres in height in its natural habitat. The metre-wide fronds are arranged in a spreading crown which has a diameter of nearly 12 metres. Foliage is a beautiful soft green. Essentially a garden species, it will nevertheless adapt well to container culture, though growth will be slower and size reduced.

Outside, the plant prefers light shade and will benefit from the regular misting of its trunk. If cultivated in a container, it should be repotted in spring, when new fronds begin to appear. Cut withered leaves off close to the trunk.
Propagation: from spores.

Cyathea capensis/Alsophila capensis
Forest Tree Fern

This species is found in various parts of South Africa, but can also be found in scattered localities as far northwards as Tanzania. It is a beautifully graceful fern with a caudex up to 4,5 metres in height and 10 cm in diameter. The plant carries from 5 to 7 fronds at one time, these ranging between 1,5 metres and 3 metres long. Modified pinnae appear as a hair-like mat within the crown and these act as a moisture trap.

The Forest Tree Fern requires high humidity at all times and is very sensitive to frost and wind damage. In its natural state it occurs in moist, shaded ravines. It may not, however, always be readily available to the home gardener.
Propagation: from spores.

Cyathea dregei/Alsophila dregei
Common Tree Fern

This species is found in a few areas of South Africa and the Transkei, and also in fairly heavy concentrations in Lesotho, Swaziland, Zimbabwe and Mozambique. It is an outstanding fern with a caudex up to 5 metres in height and 45 cm in diameter. The arching fronds, which measure up to 1,5 metres in length and between 60 cm and 90 cm in breadth, are arranged in a crown at the top of the caudex and, from a distance, slightly resemble the ancient cycad.

Once established, the Common Tree Fern will tolerate full sun, but here it will be smaller and not so luxuriant; it thrives in semi-shade. Water the plants regularly and, at the same time, hose down the caudex. It is very important to keep the ground moist around the fern. Remove old fronds as they die off.
Propagation: from spores.

1 *Blechnum australe*
2 *Blechnum gibbum*
3 Mountain Blechnum
4 Australian Tree Fern
5 Forest Tree Fern
6 Common Tree Fern

Cyrtomium falcatum
Holly Fern

Indigenous to Asia and Polynesia, the pinnae of this lustrous, dark-green fern have saw-toothed margins, somewhat reminiscent of holly, and hence its common name. Under favourable conditions the fronds can grow to a length of 75 cm. It is one of the easiest ferns to cultivate for, although it comes from the tropics, it will tolerate a wide range of conditions, including temperature extremes. It does, however, prefer a fairly acid soil and light shade. It is a striking plant for indoors, but can also be grown in gardens, including warmer gardens in cool temperate areas.

Propagation: this is quite easy from spores, especially if the pot is placed on a large drip tray filled with moist sand and peat; spores will drift down when ripe and should germinate in the sand mixture.

Davallia bullata
Rabbit's-foot Fern

Native to Asia, this fern derives its name from the creeping rhizomes which grow over the sides of pots, and look somewhat like rabbits' feet covered in hairs. It is a pretty plant, with finely divided fronds, and is ideal for growing in hanging baskets as the rhizomes soon fill the container and creep over the edges. It can be grown outdoors in warm temperate areas under trees, in the ground or in large, flat containers filled with a suitable soil mixture (see page 4). If grown in open ground, the soil should drain easily and be well prepared.

The species is technically deciduous, but new growth will appear before the old fronds drop off, so for practical – or rather, visual – purposes it can be regarded as an evergreen. It is also a fairly hardy plant, tolerating a wide temperature range and, indoors, grows well in both low and bright light. Repot in spring when new growth begins.

Propagation: from spores, or by division of the creeping rhizomes.

Doryopteris pedata
Hand Fern

Indigenous to the New World tropical regions, this small fern is n often seen, but is in fact grown, in this country. The infertile from look somewhat like maple leaves; the fertile leaves have the sam shape but are divided up into leaflets. The colour of both the inferti and fertile foliage changes from light to dark green as the plant m tures, and the stalk changes from light green to a polished bla colour. When grown indoors, this fern needs a very good light, a must be kept moist but not sodden.

Propagation: from spores; by division – pegging buds to the surfa of a moist potting compound; or from bulblets.

Dryopteris inaequalis

This is an attractive fern that belongs to a genus comprising at lea 150 species; nine of these occur in South Africa. It is rare in the We ern Cape, but occurrence increases farther eastwards and nort wards, with good distributions in Natal, Lesotho and the Transva Beyond those northern areas the plant becomes a lot less common. is usually found in forests, where conditions are shady and moist. swampy ground it can reach a height of 1,8 metres, but generally not more than a metre tall. Mid-green, deeply cut and much-divid fronds make it an attractive fern for shaded parts of tropical garde In very dry areas the fern is dormant during the driest periods, th showing a seasonal pattern of growth; but in areas where rainfall high it will remain green throughout the year.

The rhizome of *D. inaequalis* is erect or creeping and fronds emer from the crown or growing tip. The plant is strong and easily cul vated but it does need to be kept consistently moist without being lowed to become waterlogged. Indoors, the fern will thrive in a c place, in bright but indirect light.

Propagation: from spores.

2

3

4

Marsilea
Water Clover; Clover ferns

There are 65 species in this genus which are distributed over the temperate and tropical regions of the world; about a dozen are found in South Africa. They are all small plants (from 7,5 cm to 15 cm, depending on where they grow) and aquatic or semi-aquatic, requiring seasonal or permanent submergence in water. Fronds are divided into four and arranged in the shape of a cross, somewhat like a clover leaf. Outdoors, Water Clover can be grown on the edges of fish ponds, where the soil is marshy, or in the fish pond itself. The plants spread readily in favourable conditions, and thrive in both open shade and full sunlight. Indoors, they are suitable for growing in shallow pots (and should be kept very wet), or in aquariums and terrariums. In tropical regions they favour direct sun, or bright indirect light.

Propagation: by division of the rootstock, or from spores – these are produced within a *sporocarp*: a small, bean-shaped structure produced at rhizome level at the base of stipes. In drought conditions the plants survive in the form of sporocarps.

1 Holly Fern (foreground)
2 Rabbit's-foot Fern
3 Hand Fern
4 *Dryopteris inaequalis*
5 Water Clover

5

NEPHROLEPIS

The species in this genus are commonly known as Sword ferns. Because of their good nature and their attractive foliage, they are very popular as indoor plants. Probably the most renowned of them is the natural mutant *Nephrolepis exaltata* 'Bostoniensis': the Boston Fern, of which there are a number of cultivars.

All the *Nephrolepis* ferns need water regularly, but should be allowed to dry slightly between waterings. From early spring until the end of summer, they will benefit from the application (once a month) of Maxicrop seaweed feed at half-strength. Keep the plants neat by trimming off old fronds as they turn yellow, and unless the stolons are needed for propagation, trim them off as well.

Propagation: from spores, by pegging down stolons, or by division of the crowns.

Nephrolepis cordifolia
Sword Fern; Fishbone Fern

This species, which has undivided pinnae all the way up the rachids, is the easiest to grow of the genus. It can be grown indoors, where it prefers a low level of indirect light (though it is quite happy in bright light), or outdoors in tropical gardens, where it will tolerate both shade and sun.

The plant should be kept fairly moist, but the soil is best left to dry out a little between waterings. Cultivated in a container, it will be at its best when the roots fill (without crowding) their pot.

The Fishbone Fern has a number of attractive cultivars, including 'Duffii' – a smaller but attractive fern and 'Tesellata' which is also suitable for display.

Nephrolepis exaltata 'Bostoniensis'
Boston Fern

This is a natural mutant of the Sword Fern which has produced some outstanding cultivars of its own:

'Boston Gold' is the latest introduction. It has strikingly golden-coloured foliage, and makes a lovely sight in a large shallow bowl. The plant can be seen to particular advantage if grouped, for startling contrast, with green ferns. 'Boston Gold' needs strong light.

'Dallas' has a compact habit of growth and dark green foliage. 'Fluffy Ruffles', with its fine foliage, is one of the most beautiful and most popular of the cultivars, which looks best growing down from a hanging basket, or in a large pot in a palm-stand. 'Rooseveltii' has long fronds, ruffled towards the tips, and is another excellent plant for hanging baskets. 'Teddy Junior' also has long fronds which are ruffled, but not so distinctively as 'Fluffy Ruffles'.

Osmunda regalis
Royal Fern

This species, distributed world-wide, is especially interesting to botanists, as it provides a link between the ancient forests of ferns that once carpeted the earth, and the fern plants familiar to us today. It is nearly always located along river-banks and streams, growing in half to full shade, rarely in the open. These conditions are ideal for the plant and should be matched as far as possible when it is cultivated in the garden. Out of doors, where it makes an exceptionally attractive feature, the fern can reach a height of 1,8 m in cool temperate as well as tropical gardens.

The Royal Fern is also suitable for container culture, but will occasionally require transplanting into a larger pot in order to accommodate the expanding root system. In time, however, it will probably have to be planted out in the garden when it becomes too large for the house or patio.

Propagation: from spores (which have a very short viability) in early summer, or by division of crowns in spring, just before new growth begins. The divisions should be planted 90 cm apart.

1

2

1 Sword Fern
2 Boston Fern cultivar, 'Rooseveltii'
3 Boston Fern

Pellaea rotundifolia
Button Fern

Indigenous to New Zealand, this is an unusual fern with characteristic button-shaped pinnae. It has medium-creeping and wiry rhizomes, dark stipes, and small fronds which form an attractive clump. The plant prefers slightly alkaline soil, and fairly dry conditions; keep the soil on the dry side of moist, as overwatering can kill it. The Button Fern can be cultivated outdoors in warm temperate areas, but must be protected from slugs and snails, and from excessive rainfall. It also makes an attractive indoor fern, in a pot or hanging basket, where it prefers low indirect light.

Propagation: from spores, or by division of rhizomes in spring, before new growth begins.

Pityrogramma calomelanos var. aureoflava
Gold Fern; Goldback Fern

This is an interesting evergreen plant, with fronds that grow from 30 cm to 90 cm. The original species came from South America, but the plant has become established in South Africa, and in the Old World tropics. It is found in the wet crevices of rocks in the countryside, and between bricks and cracks in stone walls. The plant gets its common name from the yellow 'gold dust' on the backs of the fronds. In the wild, the Gold Fern thrives under high rainfall and half to full shade; if cultivated in the garden, therefore, it will need plenty of shade and moisture. Indoors, the plant prefers bright indirect light.

Propagation: from spores, or by division in spring, before new growth begins.

4   Button Fern
5   Royal Fern
6   Gold Fern

Platycerium bifurcatum
Stag's-horn Fern

One of the epiphytic ferns, this particular species comes from tropical Australia, and many varieties and cultivars are now available. It is an impressive fern, the fertile 'stag's-horn' fronds being set against a background of sterile fronds. The spore masses appear as a soft brown fuzz on the backs of the tips of the mature 'antlers'.

Although epiphytic, these plants can be grown in pots. However, they look more attractive when attached to a block of wood, bark or piece of tree branch. In warm areas they can be grown outside on trees. The plants require bright indirect light.

In summer, these ferns should be watered well twice a week, and misted down; in winter, water once a week. Feed twice a year, in spring and mid-summer, with Maxicrop seaweed feed at half strength. Do not remove old sterile brown fronds as these trap falling leaves and other matter which decays and provides the plant with nutrients; the old foliage also serves as a moisture trap.

Propagation: from spores which are produced seasonally; or by taking out and rooting the small plants that develop beneath the basal fronds.

Polystichum
Shield ferns

There are about 200 species of ferns in this family, all robust ferns but with variable forms. They are native to the temperate regions, and about six are indigenous to South Africa. All Shield ferns prefer soil which is kept constantly moist but never soggy. Bright indirect light is favoured, and temperatures ideally range between 7° C and 13° C in winter, and from 18° C to 24° C in the summer months. Certain species can be grown out of doors, while all Shield ferns make elegant indoor plants.

Do not feed recently purchased or repotted plants, but fertilize ones that are established with Maxicrop seaweed feed at half strength in spring and summer.

Propagation: from spores, or by division of crowns in spring.

Pteridium aquilinum
Bracken

Bracken, distributed world-wide, is a pernicious weed in Britain which should on no account be deliberately planted in gardens, as it is not possible for gardeners to destroy it. It is a tough plant, with rough, leathery, triangular fronds growing to between 30 cm and 60 cm in both length and width. It is not too popular in country districts, as it can quickly invade large tracts of land and is then difficult to eradicate. Bracken is not a favourite with farmers either, as the leaves are toxic and, eaten in large amounts by grazing cattle, will destroy Vitamin B1 reserves. A useful fern, however, when planted as a fairly tall (knee-high) ground cover for otherwise bleak parts of a large property. It will tolerate almost any soil and light condition, but prefers a slightly dry bed and open shade.

Propagation: easily from spores, and also by division of the underground stem. Bracken does not transplant easily.

1

2

3

PTERIS

The species of this genus are, generally speaking, easy to grow, adaptable, and make excellent house-plants. The larger ones are often used as floor-displays in office blocks and other public buildings. Numerous decorative cultivars are available. The lowest pair of leaflets on all *Pteris* species are divided, producing a butterfly effect.

Outdoors, this group of ferns needs a consistently moist but never soggy soil, and all enjoy light shade. Indoors, bright indirect light, and fairly humid conditions are favoured. Minimum temperature is 13° C.

Propagation: from spores, or by division of the plant's base.

Pteris cretica 'Albo-lineata'
Ribbon Fern

This is a beautiful, shapely, small fern with a distinctive, broad cream stripe running down the centre of the pinnae. One of the most hardy members of the genus, it does best in good indirect light, and must be kept well watered. Outdoors, it makes an attractive individual display, but should be placed in a sheltered and lightly shaded position.

Pteris ensiformis/P. crenata
Sword Brake Fern

This fern is indigenous to eastern Asia, Malasia and Australia. It has two types of fronds which differ in appearance from each other – the infertile ones, measuring 25 cm to 45 cm in length, have elliptical leaflets, while the fertile ones are erect and wavy-edged. The cultivar 'Victoriae' is as attractive a fern with silvery-white stripes down the centres of its pinnae.

Pteris tremula
Table Fern; Tender Brake Fern; Trembling Fern

This fern has a delicate structure, and a literally trembling appearance. Mature specimens can grow to a metre and more in height, and have deeply lobed, overlapping and rather coarse leaflets. The young plants make very appealing indoor displays and the adults make attractive floor plants. The fronds of the Table Fern are useful for cut foliage in an indoor arrangement.

1   Stag's-horn Fern
2   Bracken
3   *Polystichum lucidum* (an indigenous Shield Fern)
4   Ribbon Fern
5   Table Fern
6   Sword Brake Fern

Rumohra adiantiformis
Knysna Fern; Leather Leaf Fern; Seven Week Fern

The Knysna Fern is indigenous to the tropical and warm temperate regions of the southern hemisphere, and is usually located in shady forests or forest margins, or in rocky ravines. The stipe (stalk) of the frond grows to anything between 30 cm and 80 cm in length, and the fronds, which are leathery, can reach a length and width of 70 cm. It is an attractive fern, suitable for the shady, moist parts of a tropical or warm temperate garden, and prefers a well-drained soil with a high humus content. The fronds last extremely well in water, as the third of the common names indicates.

Propagation: from spores, or by division of the rhizome.

Todea barbara/Todea africana

This shrub-sized fern is found in warm temperate areas of southern Africa, Australia and New Zealand.

Todea barbara is an attractive fern, much larger than most of the decorative ferns, but not quite as large as the tree ferns. The thick stem, up to 1 m high, gives rise to a mass of leathery fronds – usually 1 m long but which under very damp and shady conditions may be as long as 1,5 m and more. This fern thrives in shade and prefers a soil which is acidic, damp and well-drained. It makes an appealing feature plant in a shaded garden bed, but also grows well in a container. A young specimen can be grown indoors in very bright indirect sunlight, and requires soil which is constantly moist, but never soggy.

Propagation: from spores or by dividing plants.

1   *Todea barbara*
2   Knysna Fern

1

2